The Book of **Tree Poems**

LAURENCE KING

First published in Great Britain in 2023
by Laurence King Publishing
an imprint of The Orion Publishing Group Ltd
Carmelite House, 50 Victoria Embankment
London EC4Y 0DZ

An Hachette UK Company

10 9 8 7 6 5 4 3 2 1

A CIP catalogue record for this book is available
from the British Library.

ISBN 978 1 39960 909 8

Commissioning editor: Andrew Roff
Senior editor: Laura Paton
Design: Hannah Owens
Poetry clearance: Clear Permissions

Origination by F1 Colour Ltd, London
Printed in China by C&C Offset Printing Co. Ltd

www.laurenceking.com
www.orionbooks.co.uk

The Book of **Tree Poems**

Sarah Maycock & Ana Sampson

Laurence King Publishing

Contents

Introduction

'Heaven and earth help him who plants a tree,
And his work its own reward shall be.'
Lucy Larcom

It is hard to write about trees *without* writing poetry.
From the most ancient times, in every corner of the
world, we have plaited them into our stories. The pagan
hearth was festooned with evergreen branches to resist
the winter's darkness, and we still sense some urgent
magic in the air each spring when blossom bursts out
amid birdsong. Walking through an orchard sagging
with bounty, it is easy to see why our ancestors wassailed
and worshipped their fruit trees. Trees have offered us
shelter, shade and ships, fruit and flowers, life itself.
From Eden's tree of knowledge to the Norse world
tree Yggdrasil, from the Māori forest god Tāne to the
Buddha's banyan, trees have been holy to us forever –
and they are still.

Trees mark our time for us. Resplendent in summer
green or autumn crimson, stark against a frosty sky or
gleefully igniting with bud and blossom in the spring,
they root us in the landscape and plant us firmly in
the present. It can be hard to see the summer die,
but for many of us the blazing colours of October are
consolation enough – a harvest-time invitation to drink
in the last golden hours before winter dawns. And when

spring comes again, as it must, trees have spoken to so many of the poets gathered in this volume of resilience, making promises to, as Larkin says, 'Begin afresh, afresh, afresh.'

Some of these trees are more than trees. Ruth Awolola and Walt Whitman are told something about themselves by the trees they think and write about. For Anna Wickham, her life is an ancient tree 'And the young buds are your sweet love for me.' It is hard to rest beneath a tree and not to feel contemplative, not to feel both rooted in the earth and stretched airily above the busy, trivial world. Some of these trees, of course, are only trees. But trees can make a child catch their breath in wonder, or look at the world from a new perspective. Trees give us breath and blessings, feasts of fruit, the busy carol of the birds and the heart-lifting joy of their beauty. Trees are the land's treasure, and ours.

The poets in this collection introduce us to their personal sylvan pantheons, for trees stand as landmarks in all our lives. We meet both shivering saplings and antique giants, such as Katharine Towers' great oak – 'a galleon tilting in the moonlight.' A venerable tree inspires thoughts of the centuries it has weathered, and those who walked and dreamed beneath it long before us. We must wonder how many of Wordsworth's poems were begun under branches that made 'A twilight of their own', and what Warwickshire idyll rose in Shakespeare's mind when, perhaps, he scratched out 'Under the greenwood tree' in noisy Southwark.

In this book are gathered a chorus line of singing, dancing trees. 'I say,' writes Mandy Haggith, 'it's about listening to the trees'. And what a show they put on! From Sarah Doyle's 'flying sunshiny shower' of birch to Charles Causley's 'glancing / Dancing tree', these poets have beautifully captured the giddy exhilaration inspired by a sea of leaves waving in the wind. Their words can help us hear Sassoon's 'chant and whisper of the glade' when we cannot escape to wander in the woods ourselves. Poetry is our magic carpet.

As children, we built kingdoms among the trees. Though most of us could only envy those lucky enough to have their own treehouse, the idea of a hideaway secreted in the canopy has enduring power, springing up everywhere from *Tom's Midnight Garden* to *The Simpsons*. Whether we clambered high into the branches or looked for fairies or beetles among the roots, trees were our playgrounds. We hoarded their treasures: glossy conkers, sycamore spinners, cherry stones, acorn cups for tiny feasts, tumbled blossom, sticky buds to uncurl in a milk bottle. They furnished us with swords, pilgrims' staffs and magic wands. They were milestones and boundaries, and a certain well-loved tree might have been – might still be – the landmark that tells us: "You are home." In ever-changing landscapes, it is like meeting an old friend to see a remembered tree spreading its quiet arms over new houses. We feel a true grief to lose them.

Within my private forest of remembered trees stand a friendly magnolia, regularly scrambled up in childhood, and the horse chestnut – in my mind, always bearing its pale candles – visible from a window I last gazed from decades ago. Further in, a hilltop monkey puzzle stretches its sinuous fingers, a neighbourhood cherry blossom blazes, an ancient oak spreads and every Christmas tree I have ever loved (which is all of them, even the scrawny ones) shines.

To lie, once in a while, under a tree and look up through its leaves is a pure and primeval kind of medicine. The air moving in the branches and the birds carolling on the boughs speak an incantation we feel we have always known, as people long before us knew it. What could we not face in this frantic world if we could be assured of a dose of this magic more often? For the times when the forest is too far away, when the rain is lashing down or the diary overflowing, I offer you these verses. Here are branches under which to rest, for a moment, and trees under which to walk. Here is a road through the woods. Turn the page, and take the first step.

Ana Sampson

Plant a Tree

Lucy Larcom (1824–1893)

He who plants a tree
    Plants a hope.
    Rootlets up through fibres blindly grope;
Leaves unfold into horizons free.
    So man's life must climb
    From the clods of time
    Unto heavens sublime
Canst thou prophesy, thou little tree,
What the glory of thy boughs shall be?

He who plants a tree
    Plants a joy;
    Plants a comfort that will never cloy;
Every day a fresh reality,
    Beautiful and strong,
    To whose shelter throng
    Creatures blithe with song.
If thou couldst but know, thou happy tree,
Of the bliss that shall inhabit thee!

He who plants a tree, –
    He plants peace.
    Under its green curtains jargons cease.
Leaf and zephyr murmur soothingly;
    Shadows soft with sleep
    Down tired eyelids creep,

Balm of slumber deep.
Never hast thou dreamed, thou blessèd tree,
Of the benediction thou shalt be.

He who plants a tree, –
　　He plants youth;
　　Vigor won for centuries in sooth;
Life of time, that hints eternity!
　　Boughs their strength uprear;
　　New shoots, every year,
　　On old growths appear;
Thou shalt teach the ages, sturdy tree,
Youth of soul is immortality.

He who plants a tree, –
　　He plants love,
　　Tents of coolness spreading out above
Wayfarers he may not live to see.
　　Gifts that grow are best;
　　Hands that bless are blest;
　　Plant! life does the rest!
Heaven and earth help him who plants
　　a tree,
And his work its own reward shall be.

On Forgetting That I Am a Tree

Ruth Awolola (b. 1998)

A poem in which I am growing.

A poem in which I am a tree,
And I am both appreciated and undervalued.

A poem in which I fear I did not dig into the past,
Did not think about my roots,
Forgot what it meant to be planted.

A poem in which I realize they may try to cut me down,
That I must change with the seasons,
That I do it so well
It looks like they are changing with me.

A poem in which I remember I have existed for centuries,
That centuries are far too small a unit of measurement,
That time found itself in the forests, woods and jungles.
Remember I have witnessed creation,
That I am key to it.

A poem in which some will carve their names into my skin
In hopes the universe will know them.
Where I am so tall I kiss the sun.
Trees cannot hide,
They belong to the day and to the night,
To the past and the future.

A poem in which I stop looking for it,
Because I am home.
I am habitat.
My branches are host and shelter
I am life-giver and fruit-bearer.
Self-sufficient protection.

A poem in which I remember I am a tree.

Loveliest of Trees, the Cherry Now

A. E. Housman (1859–1936)

Loveliest of trees, the cherry now
Is hung with bloom along the bough,
And stands about the woodland ride
Wearing white for Eastertide.

Now, of my threescore years and ten,
Twenty will not come again,
And take from seventy springs a score,
It only leaves me fifty more.

And since to look at things in bloom
Fifty springs are little room,
About the woodlands I will go
To see the cherry hung with snow.

from Oak

Katharine Towers (b. 1961)

darkness suits an old oak
which is a galleon tilting in the moonlight
like a Doré engraving

washed up in every sense of the word
an *objet trouvé*
both strange and everyday

and the bats are black suits
drawing imaginary lines
round and around

so they know where to come back to

this is the time for a very old oak to look back
to its heyday of flexing in the wind
of tossing birds up into the air
and catching them again
of flourishing greenly
and of the great meadow blowing
(cheery heads of knapweed cranesbill thistle)
of the lovely washing rain
of the last leaves coppering and dropping
making a sound like cutlery

easy then to be alive
and oh so very ordinary

Leaving Messages in Trees

Helen Burke (1953–2019)

As a child, a fanciful child – (still am)
I used to leave messages in trees.
And with the message, a small acorn and perhaps
a flower. A sprig of blossom, a forget-me-not.
The tallest tree – a big old oak on Low Moor –
a real battler – always had the most to say.
I used to leave the best message there – because I thought
this wise old self held most of the answers.
(Seeking answers, even then.)
Mam would help me place it there, and wait further down
the hill while I said my tree prayer.
But trees know better than to give response – only the sky
above them and the roots below the sky will they speak of.
And this is as it should be.
'The skies, roots and the bird that lives in the moon – they
sing. Let this be our answer to you.
Now away with you.'
Only once – a piece of paper (Mam's writing) 'I Love You'.
And this the answer that I treasure.
And this the answer that I keep.

Green Rain

Mary Webb (1881–1927)

Into the scented woods we'll go,
And see the blackthorn swim in snow.
High above, in the budding leaves,
A brooding dove awakes and grieves;
The glades with mingled music stir,
And wildly laughs the woodpecker.
When blackthorn petals pearl the breeze,
There are the twisted hawthorn trees
Thick-set with buds, as clear and pale
As golden water or green hail –
As if a storm of rain had stood
Enchanted in the thorny wood,
And, hearing fairy voices call,
Hung poised, forgetting how to fall.

Moved by the Beauty of Trees

Ishion Hutchinson (b. 1983)

The beauty of the trees stills her;
she is stillness staring at the leaves,

still and green and keeping up the sky;
their beauty stills her and she is quiet

in her stare, her eyes' long lashes curve
and keep, her little mouth opens

and keeps still with its quiet for the beauty
of the trees, their leaves, the sky

and its blue quiet, very still and quiet;
her looking eyes wide, deep, silent

hard on the trees and the beauty
of the sky, the green of the leaves.

Untitled

Anryū Suharu

When, with breaking heart,
I realize
this world is only a dream,
the oak tree looks radiant.

from The Recollection

Percy Bysshe Shelley (1792–1822)

Now the last day of many days
All beautiful and bright as thou,
The loveliest and the last, is dead,
Rise, Memory, and write its praise!
Up, do they wonted work! come, trace
The epitaph of glory fled,
For now the Earth has changed its face,
A frown is on the Heaven's brow.

We wander'd to the Pine Forest
    That skirts the Ocean's foam;
The lightest wind was in its nest,
    The tempest in its home.
The whispering waves were half asleep,
    The clouds were gone to play,
And on the bosom of the deep
    The smile of Heaven lay;
It seem'd as if the hour were one
    Sent from beyond the skies
Which scatter'd from above the sun
    A light of Paradise!

We paused amid the pines that stood
    The giants of the waste,
Tortured by storms to shapes as rude
    As serpents interlaced, –

And soothed by every azure breath
    That under heaven is blown
To harmonies and hues beneath,
    As tender as its own:
Now all the tree-tops lay asleep
    Like green waves on the sea,
As still as in the silent deep
    The ocean-woods may be.

How calm it was! – the silence there
    By such a chain was bound,
That even the busy woodpecker
    Made stiller by her sound
The inviolable quietness;
    The breath of peace we drew
With its soft motion made not less
    The calm that round us grew.
There seem'd from the remotest seat
    Of the wide mountain waste
To the soft flower beneath our feet
    A magic circle traced,
A spirit interfused around,
    A thrilling silent life;
To momentary peace it bound
    Our mortal nature's strife; –
And still I felt the centre of
    The magic circle there
Was one fair Form that fill'd with love
    The lifeless atmosphere.

Trees

Alfred Joyce Kilmer (1886–1918)

I think that I shall never see
A poem lovely as a tree.

A tree whose hungry mouth is prest
Against the earth's sweet flowing breast;

A tree that looks at God all day,
And lifts her leafy arms to pray;

A tree that may in Summer wear
A nest of robins in her hair;

Upon whose bosom snow has lain;
Who intimately lives with rain.

Poems are made by fools like me,
But only God can make a tree.

The Awakening

Anna Wickham (1883–1947)

There is a veteran tree,
With green-stained bark,
Rising like a tower of the sea,
From the smooth park.
He is a giant among trees,
And he has watched this house for centuries.

His bark is hard as rock,
Time and Sun and the Wind's shock
Have twisted his boughs till they are like the
    arms of a great carven figure of Care,
Flung in passionate appeal to the changing
    humour of the Air.
Now on high branches sticky buds appear,
Promise of growth and beauty for the year.
It seems my life is an old tree,
And the young buds are your sweet love for me.

The Purple Peach Tree

Su Tung P'o (1037–1101)

Timidly, still half asleep, it has blossomed.
Afraid of the teeth of the frost, it was late this year.
Now its crimson mixes with the
Brilliance of the cherries and apricots.
Unique, it is more beautiful than snow and hoar frost.
Under the cold, its heart awoke to the Spring season.
Full of wine, sprawling on the alabaster table,
I dream of the ancient poet who could not distinguish
The peach, the cherry and the apricot, except by their
Green leaves and dark branches.

Child's Song in Spring

Edith Nesbit (1858–1924)

The Silver Birch is a dainty lady,
She wears a satin gown;
The elm tree makes the old churchyard shady,
She will not live in town.

The English oak is a sturdy fellow,
He gets his green coat late;
The willow is smart in a suit of yellow
While brown the beech trees wait.

Such a gay green gown God gives the larches –
As green as he is good!
The hazels hold up their arms for arches,
When spring rides through the wood.

The chestnut's proud, and the lilac's pretty,
The poplar's gentle and tall,
But the plane tree's kind to the poor dull city –
I love him best of all!

Under Silver How

Sarah Doyle

As we were going along we were stopped
at once, at the distance perhaps of 50 yards
from our favourite birch tree. It was yielding
to the gusty wind with all its tender twigs.

The sun shone upon it, and it glanced
in the wind like a flying sunshiny shower.
It was a tree in shape, with stem and branches,
but it was like a spirit of water. The sun went

in, and it resumed its purplish appearance,
the twigs still yielding to the wind, but not
so visibly to us. The other birch trees
that were near it looked bright and cheerful,

but it was a creature by its own self among them.

In May

Alison Brackenbury (b. 1953)

The Cox's apple tree has blowsy swags,
a girl's bare shoulders, falling from a dress.
Hawthorn, though held bad luck, shines pale and neat,
a distant housewife, waving off her guest.
Untrimmed and unplanted, worn by weather,
one small tree's flowers burn red, unperplexed,
flash snow. Crab apples, in pale yellow pools
like sun, feed all, split, patient, wait the next.

Listening to the Trees

Mandy Haggith

And the birch says
      it's about dancing and colour

and the rowan says
      it's about berries and birds

and the willow says
      it's about shape and shelter

and the hazel says
      it's about love and lichen

and the aspen says
      it's about growth and the wind

but I say it's about
      listening to the trees

I Saw in Louisiana a Live-Oak Growing

Walt Whitman (1819–1892)

I saw in Louisiana a live-oak growing,
All alone stood it and the moss hung down from the
   branches,
Without any companion it grew there uttering joyous
   leaves of dark green,
And its look, rude, unbending, lusty, made me think of
   myself,
But I wonder'd how it could utter joyous leaves
   standing alone there without its friend near, for
   I knew I could not,
And I broke off a twig with a certain number of leaves
   upon it, and twined around it a little moss,
And brought it away, and I have placed it in sight in
   my room,
It is not needed to remind me as of my own dear
   friends,
(For I believe lately I think of little else than of them,)
Yet it remains to me a curious token, it makes me
   think of manly love;
For all that, and though the live-oak glistens there in
   Louisiana solitary in a wide flat space,
Uttering joyous leaves all its life without a friend
   a lover near,
I know very well I could not.

The Trees

Philip Larkin (1922–1985)

The trees are coming into leaf
Like something almost being said;
The recent buds relax and spread,
Their greenness is a kind of grief.

Is it that they are born again
And we grow old? No, they die too.
Their yearly trick of looking new
Is written down in rings of grain.

Yet still the unresting castles thresh
In fullgrown thickness every May.
Last year is dead, they seem to say,
Begin afresh, afresh, afresh.

Not Dead

Robert Graves (1895–1985)

Walking through trees to cool my
heat and pain,
I know that David's with me here
again.
All that is simple, happy, strong, he
is.
Caressingly I stroke
Rough bark of the friendly oak.
A brook goes bubbling by: the voice
is his.
Turf burns with pleasant smoke;
I laugh at chaffinch and at
primroses.
All that is simple, happy, strong, he
is.
Over the whole wood in a little
while
Breaks his slow smile.

Staying Overnight
at Xiaosha Stream

Yang Wanli (1127–1206)

Trees, laced in mountain mist,
    patch broken clouds;
the wind scatters a rainstorm of fragrant petals.
The green willows, it is said, are without feeling –
why then do they try so hard to touch the traveller
    with their catkins?

Climbing

Amy Lowell (1874–1925)

High up in the apple tree climbing I go,
With the sky above me, the earth below.
Each branch is the step of a wonderful stair
Which leads to the town I see shining up there.

Climbing, climbing, higher and higher,
The branches blow and I see a spire,
The gleam of a turret, the glint of a dome,
All sparkling and bright, like white sea foam.

On and on, from bough to bough,
The leaves are thick, but I push my way through;
Before, I have always had to stop,
But to-day I am sure I shall reach the top.

Today to the end of the marvelous stair,
Where those glittering pinacles flash in the air!
Climbing, climbing, higher I go,
With the sky close above me, the earth far below.

Trees of Song

Pascale Petit (b. 1953)

You call us the trees of song
        because when night falls
                we draw the bows of our branches

against our trunks
        and play for our lives.
                When the forest gates open

we let you in,
        start our day's work
                making air, growing wombs

that dream up birds.
        It is we who are singing
                the leopard and langur,

replacing the ones you kill.
        You come dressed as a groom
                all in red

with rifles for branches
            as if you could marry
                    your green bride.

We sing the hymns that burn
            at the centre of the earth.
                    We call them up

and they surge through us.
            Our bows play so fast
                    we self-combust

like brides who don't want to marry,
            who set themselves alight.
                    By sunrise all you see

is smoke rising from our stumps
            like morning mist,
                    and our spirits are gone.

In My Garden

Charles Causley (1917–2003)

In my garden
Grows a tree
Dances day
And night for me,
Four in a bar
Or sometimes three
To music secret
As can be.

Nightly to
Its hidden tune
I watch it move
Against the moon,
Dancing to
A silent sound,
One foot planted
In the ground.

Dancing tree,
When may I hear
Day or night
Your music clear?
What the note
And what the song
That you sing
The seasons long?

It is written
Said the tree,
On the pages
Of the sea;
It is there
At every hand
On the pages
Of the land;

Whether waking
Or in dream:
Voice of meadow-grass
And stream,
And out of
The ringing air
Voice of sun
And moon and star.

It is there
For all to know
As tides shall turn
And wildflowers grow;
There for you
And there for me,
Said the glancing
Dancing tree.

The Trees' Counselling

Christina Rossetti (1830–1894)

I was strolling sorrowfully
    Thro' the corn fields and the meadows;
The stream sounded melancholy,
    And I walked among the shadows;
While the ancient forest trees
Talked together in the breeze;
In the breeze that waved and blew them,
With a strange weird rustle thro' them.

Said the oak unto the others
    In a leafy voice and pleasant:
'Here we all are equal brothers,
    'Here we have nor lord nor peasant.
'Summer, Autumn, Winter, Spring,
'Pass in happy following.
'Little winds may whistle by us,
'Little birds may overfly us;

'But the sun still waits in heaven
    'To look down on us in splendour;
'When he goes the moon is given,
    'Full of rays that he doth lend her:
'And tho' sometimes in the night
'Mists may hide her from our sight,
'She comes out in the calm weather,
'With the glorious stars together.'

From the fruitage, from the blossom,
　　From the trees came no denying;
Then my heart said in my bosom:
　　'Wherefore art thou sad and sighing?
'Learn contentment from this wood
'That proclaimeth all states good;
'Go not from it as it found thee;
'Turn thyself and gaze around thee.'

And I turned: behold the shading
　　But showed forth the light more clearly;
The wild bees were honey-lading;
　　The stream sounded hushing merely,
And the wind not murmuring
Seemed, but gently whispering;
'Get thee patience; and thy spirit
'Shall discern in all things merit.'

Wind in the Beechwood

Siegfried Sassoon (1886–1967)

The glorying forest shakes and swings with glancing
Of boughs that dip and strain; young, slanting sprays
Beckon and shift like lissom creatures dancing,
While the blown beechwood streams with drifting rays.
    Rooted in steadfast calm, grey stems are seen
    Like weather-beaten masts; the wood, unfurled,
    Seems as a ship with crowding sails of green
    That sweeps across the lonely billowing world.

O luminous and lovely! Let your flowers,
Your ageless-squadroned wings, your surge and gleam,
Drown me in quivering brightness: let me fade
    In the warm, rustling music of the hours
    That guard your ancient wisdom, till my dream
    Moves with the chant and whisper of the glade.

The Green Roads

Edward Thomas (1878–1917)

The green roads that end in the forest
Are strewn with white goose feathers this June,

Like marks left behind by someone gone to the forest
To show his track. But he has never come back.

Down each green road a cottage looks at the forest.
Round one the nettle towers; two are bathed in flowers.

An old man along the green road to the forest
Strays from one, from another a child alone.

In the thicket bordering the forest,
All day long a thrush twiddles his song.

It is old, but the tress are young in the forest,
All but one like a castle keep, in the middle deep.

That oak saw the ages pass in the forest:
They were a host, but their memories are lost,

For the tree is dead: all things forget the forest
Excepting perhaps me, when now I see

The old man, the child, the goose feathers at the edge
    of the forest,
And hear all day long the thrush repeat his song.

The World of Trees

Jackie Kay (b. 1961)

Sycamore. Mountain Ash. Beech. Birch. Oak.

In the middle of the forest the trees stood.
And the beech knew the birch was there.
And the mountain ash breathed the same air
as the sycamore, and everywhere

the wind blew, the trees understood each other:
How the river made the old oak lean to the east,
how the felled beech changed the currents of the wind,
how the two common ash formed a canapé,

and grew in a complementary way.
Between them they shared a full head of hair.
Some amber curls of the one could easily
belong to the other: twin trees, so similar.

Sycamore. Mountain Ash. Beech. Birch. Oak.

Some trees crouched in the forest waiting,
for another tree to die so that they could
shoot up suddenly in that new space;
stretch out comfortably for the blue sky.

Some trees grew mysterious mushroom fungi,
shoelace, honey, intricate as a grandmother's lace.

The wind fluttered the leaves; the leaves flapped their wings.
Birds flew from the trees. Sometimes they'd sing.

The tall trees, compassionate, understood everything:
grief – they stood stock still, branches dropped in despair.
Fear – they exposed their many roots, tugged their gold hair.
Anger – they shook in the storm, pointed their bony fingers.

Sycamore. Mountain Ash. Beech. Birch. Oak.

The trees knew each other's secrets.
In the deep green heart of the forest.
Each tree loved another tree best.
Each tree, happy to rest, lean a little to the east,

or to the west, when the moon loomed high above,
the big white eye of the woods.
And they stood together as one in the dark,
with the stars sparkling from their branches,

completely at ease, breathing in the cold night air
swishing a little in the breeze,
dreaming of glossy spring leaves
in the fine, distinguished company of trees.

Sycamore. Mountain Ash. Beech. Birch. Oak

Forest

Carol Ann Duffy (b. 1955)

There were flowers at the edge of the forest, cupping
the last light in their upturned petals. I followed you in,
under the sighing, restless trees and my whole life vanished.

The moon tossed down its shimmering cloth. We undressed,
then dressed again in the gowns of the moon. We knelt in the
     leaves,
kissed, kissed; new words rustled nearby and we swooned.

Didn't we? And didn't I see you rise again and go deeper
into the woods and follow you still, till even my
     childhood shrank
to a glow-worm of light where those flowers darkened
     and closed.

Thorns on my breast, rain in my mouth, loam on my bare
     feet, rough
bark grazing my back, I moaned for them all. You stood,
     waist deep,
in a stream, pulling me in, so I swam. You were the
     water, the wind

in the branches wringing their hands, the heavy, wet
     perfume of soil.
I am there now, lost in the forest, dwarfed by the giant
     trees. Find me.

The Way Through the Woods

Rudyard Kipling (1865–1936)

They shut the road through the woods
    Seventy years ago.
Weather and rain have undone it again,
    And now you would never know
There was once a road through the woods
    Before they planted the trees.
It is underneath the coppice and heath,
    And the thin anemones.
Only the keeper sees
    That, where the ring-dove broods,
And the badgers roll at ease,
    There was once a road through the woods.

Yet, if you enter the woods
    Of a summer evening late,
When the night-air cools on the trout-ringed pools
    Where the otter whistles his mate,
(They fear not men in the woods,
    Because they see so few)
You will hear the beat of a horse's feet
    And the swish of a skirt in the dew,
    Steadily cantering through
The misty solitudes,
    As though they perfectly knew
The old lost road through the woods…
But there is no road through the woods.

Emerson

Mary Mapes Dodge (1831–1905)

We took it to the woods, we two,
    The book well worn and brown,
To read his words where stirring leaves
    Rained their soft shadows down.

Yet as we sat and breathed the scene,
    We opened not a page;
Enough that he was with us there,
    Our silent, friendly sage!

His fresh "Rhodora" bloomed again;
    His "Humble-bee" buzzed near;
And oh, the "Wood-notes" beautiful
    He taught our souls to hear.

So our unopened book was read;
    And so, in restful mood,
We and our poet, arm in arm,
    Went sauntering through the wood.

from The Marshes of Glynn

Sidney Lanier (1842–1881)

Glooms of the live-oaks, beautiful-braided and woven
With intricate shades of the vines that myriad-cloven
   Clamber the forks of the multiform boughs, –
        Emerald twilights, –
        Virginal shy lights,
Wrought of the leaves to allure to the whisper of vows,
When lovers pace timidly down through the green colonnades
   Of the dim sweet woods, of the dear dark woods,
        Of the heavenly woods and glades,
That run to the radiant marginal sand-beach within
        The wide sea-marshes of Glynn; –

   Beautiful glooms, soft dusks in the noon-day fire, –
   Wildwood privacies, closets of lone desire,
Chamber from chamber parted with wavering arras of
      leaves, –
Cells for the passionate pleasure of prayer to the soul that
      grieves,
   Pure with a sense of the passing of saints through the wood,
   Cool for the dutiful weighing of ill with good; –

O braided dusks of the oak and woven shades of the vine,
While the riotous noon-day sun of the June-day long did
      shine,

Ye held me fast in your heart and I held you fast in mine;
    But now when the noon is no more, and riot is rest,
    And the sun is a-wait at the ponderous gate of the West,
        And the slant yellow beam down the wood-aisle doth
           seem
    Like a lane into heaven that leads from a dream, –
Ay, now, when my soul all day hath drunken the soul of the
        oak,
And my heart is at ease from men, and the wearisome sound
        of the stroke
    Of the scythe of time and the trowel of trade is low,
    And belief overmasters doubt, and I know that I know,
    And my spirit is grown to a lordly great compass within,
    That the length and the breadth and the sweep of the
        marshes of Glynn
    Will work me no fear like the fear they have wrought me of
        yore
    When length was fatigue, and when breadth was but
        bitterness sore,
    And when terror and shrinking and dreary unnamable pain
    Drew over me out of the merciless miles of the plain, –
        Oh, now, unafraid, I am fain to face
           The vast sweet visage of space.

The Hollow Wood

Edward Thomas (1878-1917)

Out in the sun the goldfinch flits
Along the thistle-tops, flits and twits
Above the hollow wood
Where birds swim like fish –
Fish that laugh and shriek –
To and fro, far below
In the pale hollow wood.

Lichen, ivy, and moss
Keep evergreen the trees
That stand half-flayed and dying,
And the dead trees on their knees
In dog's-mercury, ivy, and moss:
And the bright twit of the goldfinch drops
Down there as he flits on thistle-tops.

Ash-boughs

Gerard Manley Hopkins (1844–1889)

Not of all my eyes see, wandering on the world,
Is anything a milk to the mind so, so sighs deep
Poetry to it, as a tree whose boughs break in the sky.
Say it is ash-boughs: whether on a December day and furled
Fast or they in clammyish lashtender combs creep
Apart wide and new-nestle at heaven most high.
They touch heaven, tabour on it; how their talons sweep
The smouldering enormous winter welkin! May
Mells blue and snow white through them, a fringe and fray
Of greenery: it is old earth's groping towards the steep
    Heaven whom she childs us by.

In the Woods

Kathryn Simmonds (b. 1972)

The baby sleeps.
Sunlight plays upon my lap, through doily leaves a black
  lab comes,
a scotty goes, the day wears on, the baby wakes.

The good birds sing,
Invisible or seldom seen, in hidden kingdoms, grateful
  for the in-
between. The baby sleeps. Elsewhere the Queen rolls by

on gusts of cheer –
ladies wave and bless her reign. The baby frets. The baby
  feeds.
The end of lunch, a daytime moon. The leaves

are lightly tinkered with.

It's spring? No, autumn? Afternoon? We've sat so long,
    we've walked

so far. The woods in shade, the woods in sun, the singing
    birds,

the noble trees.

The child is grown. The child is gone. The black lab
    comes,

his circuit done. His mistress coils his scarlet lead.

My Orcha'd in Linden Lea

William Barnes (1801–1886)

'Ithin the woodlands, flow'ry gleaded,
 By the woak tree's mossy moot,
The sheenen grass-bleades, timber-sheaded,
 Now do quiver under voot;
An' birds do whissle over head,
An' water's bubblen in its bed,
An' there vor me the apple tree
Do lean down low in Linden Lea.

When leaves that leately wer a-springen
 Now do feade 'ithin the copse,
An' painted birds do hush their zingen
 Up upon the timber's tops;
An' brown-leav'd fruit's a-turnen red,
In cloudless zunsheen, over head,
Wi' fruit vor me, the apple tree
Do lean down low in Linden Lea.

Let other vo'k meake money vaster
    In the air o'dark-room'd towns,
I don't dread a peevish measter;
    Though noo man do heed my frowns,
I be free to goo abrode,
Or teake agean my homeward road
To where, vor me, the apple tree
Do lean down low in Linden Lea.

Fall, Leaves, Fall

Emily Brontë (1818–1848)

Fall, leaves, fall; die, flowers away;
Lengthen night and shorten day;
Every leaf speaks bliss to me
Fluttering from the autumn tree.
I shall smile when wreaths of snow
Blossom where the rose should grow;
I shall sing when night's decay
Ushers in a drearier day.

From Blossoms

Li-Young Lee (b. 1957)

From blossoms comes
this brown paper bag of peaches
we bought from the boy
at the bend in the road where we turned toward
signs painted *Peaches.*

From laden boughs, from hands,
from sweet fellowship in the bins,
comes nectar at the roadside, succulent
peaches we devour, dusty skin and all,
comes the familiar dust of summer, dust we eat.

O, to take what we love inside,
To carry within us an orchard, to eat
not only the skin, but the shade,
not only the sugar, but the days, to hold
the fruit in our hands, adore it, then bite into
the round jubilance of peach.

There are days we live
as if death were nowhere
in the background; from joy
to joy to joy, from wing to wing,
from blossom to blossom to
impossible blossom, to sweet impossible blossom.

Flowers and Trees

Sir Walter Scott (1771–1832)

Boon nature scattered, free and wild,
Each plant or flower, the mountain's child.
Here eglantine embalmed the air,
Hawthorn and hazel mingled there;
The primrose pale, and violet flower,
Found in such cliff a narrow bower;
Fox-glove and night-shade, side by side,
Emblems of punishment and pride,
Grouped their dark hues with every stain
The weather-beaten crags retain.
With boughs that quaked at every breath,
Grey birch and aspen wept beneath;
Aloft, the ash and warrior oak
Cast anchor in the rifted rock;
And, higher yet, the pine-tree hung
His shattered trunk, and frequent flung,
Where seemed the cliffs to meet on high,
His boughs athwart the narrowed sky.
Highest of all, where white peaks glanced,
Where glistening streamers waved and danced.
The wanderer's eye could barely view
The summer heaven's delicious blue;
So wondrous wild, the whole might seem
The scenery of a fairy dream.

Summer Night, Riverside

Sara Teasdale (1884–1933)

In the wild soft summer darkness
How many and many a night we two
together
Sat in the park and watched the Hudson
Wearing her lights like golden spangles
Glinting on black satin.
The rail along the curving pathway
Was low in a happy place to let us cross,
And down the hill a tree that dripped
with bloom
Sheltered us
While your kisses and the flowers
Falling, falling,
Tangled my hair....
The frail white stars moved slowly over
the sky.

And now, far off
In the fragrant darkness
The tree is tremulous again with bloom
For June comes back.
To-night what girl
When she goes home,
Dreamily before her mirror shakes from
her hair
This year's blossoms, clinging in its coils?

The Beech Tree

Michael Longley (b. 1939)

Leaning back like a lover against this beech tree's
Two-hundred-year-old pewter trunk, I look up
Through skylights into the leafy cumulus, and join
Everybody who has teetered where these huge roots
Spread far and wide our motionless mossy dance,
As though I'd begun my eclogues with a beech
As Virgil does, the brown envelopes unfolding
Like fans their transparent downy leaves, tassels
And prickly cups, mast, a fall of vermilion
And copper and gold, then room in the branches
For the full moon and her dusty lakes, winter
And the poet who recollects his younger self
And improvises a last line for the georgics
About snoozing under this beech tree's canopy.

Under the Greenwood Tree

William Shakespeare (1564–1616)

Under the greenwood tree
Who loves to lie with me,
And tune his merry note
Unto the sweet bird's throat –
Come hither, come hither, come hither!
    Here shall we see
    No enemy
But winter and rough weather.

Who doth ambition shun
And loves to live i' the sun,
Seeking the food he eats
And pleased with what he gets –
Come hither, come hither, come hither!
Here shall he see
No enemy
But winter and rough weather.

Climbing Trees

Jason Allen-Paisant

These beeches are unclimbable
no furrows for feet

At home I knew a tree
by climbing it

Lost inside the guinep branches
I felt close to God

and I was hidden
in a place before birth

a womb
nearing the sky

For hours I would
turn into something else

one of those brown or green lizards
living up there

The limbs of an old guinep tree
are suspended walkways

you travel with your belly
with your thighs   with all your feeling

The thick muscular limb is a road
you hug   your back is a caterpillar's

legs knowing
the skin of the tree

insteps rubbing
the green moss

Travelling above the earth
I go searching for something

both tree and lizard have
to see things down below

things that never see them
folks that never think they are seen

because they never learn
to see the world from trees

The Trees

Jericho Brown (b. 1976)

In my front yard live three crape myrtles, *crying trees*
We once called them, not the shadiest but soothing
During a break from work in the heat, their cool sweat

Falling into us. I don't want to make more of it.
I'd like to let these spindly things be
Since my gift for transformation here proves

Useless now that I know everyone moves the same
Whether moving in tears or moving
To punch my face. A crape myrtle is

A crape myrtle. Three is a family. It is winter. They are bare.
It's not that I love them
Every day. It's that I love them anyway.

from The Wanderer

William Wordsworth (1770–1850)

'Twas summer, and the sun had mounted high:
Southward the landscape indistinctly glared
Through a pale steam; but all the northern downs,
In clearest air ascending, showed far off
A surface dappled o'er with shadows flung
From brooding clouds; shadows that lay in spots
Determined and unmoved, with steady beams
Of bright and pleasant sunshine interposed;
To him most pleasant who on soft cool moss
Extends his careless limbs along the front
Of some huge cave, whose rocky ceiling casts
A twilight of its own, an ample shade
Where the wren warbles, while the dreaming man,
Half conscious of the soothing melody,
With side-long eye looks out upon the scene,
By power of that impending covert, thrown
To finer distance.

The Trees Outside My Window

Moniza Alvi (b. 1954)

I'm thankful to the trees outside my window.
Only they can reach into the depth of me.
Without them, I should have died long ago –
they keep my heart alive, its eager ways.

In the long willow branches, the dark cypress,
my own ghost hides, stares out at me,
knowing me so well, pitying me in this world.
So little understanding why I stay and stay.

Orchard

Stephen Keeler (b. 1951)

I spread my shirt and lay
down in the uncut grass

a nearby orchard stood
concealed by heat and sky

the apples too lay where
they fell like redcoats shot

in battle rusting back
to earth I caught the breath

of cider on the air
the boisterous voices of

old men in corduroy
the women dressed in green

the fiddlers and the old
lament the mothers sang

before the dance before
the concertina cut

the humming air across
the hills I'd walked that day.

Moya Cannon (b. 1956)

Driving Back Over
the Blue Ridge,

you say that the leaves are late in turning.
Half way up the wooded hill to our right
the sun has decanted itself
into a single maple tree.

There are days like that
which sing orange and red
in the forest of our ordinary green.

These are the days we hang our souls upon
as high above them the sun withdraws.

For Catherine

Jen Feroze

The season is changing
sliding from sepia into sudden colour.
Gardens are splashed with birdsong.
Despite everything,
everything,
there are pockets of real sunshine.
Looking out over fens and fields,
my mind spins months hence.

Take me to the other side of summer,
please. Take me to the time when freedom
tastes familiar again.
When the meadows towards Grantchester
are speckled with walkers,
and picnic hampers
packed with the last of the sweet strawberries
and hunks of warm bread from Market Square.

Show me Rocket
shooting ahead into crunching piles
of gold and russet, paws
sending up leaves like sparks.
And later, when it's colder,
when the house begins to doze,
let my summer-stunned ideas take flight,
matching the early thunder of colour
in the darkening sky.
An explosion of chrysanthemum and sparkle,
the smell of wood and sugar on the air.

There is a Solemn Wind To-Night

Katherine Mansfield (1888–1923)

There is a solemn wind to-night
    That sings of solemn rain;
The trees that have been quiet so long
    Flutter and start again.

The slender trees, the heavy trees,
    The fruit trees laden and proud,
Lift up their branches to the wind
    That cries to them so loud.

The little bushes and the plants
    Bow to the solemn sound,
And every tiniest blade of grass
    Shakes on the quiet ground.

On the First Leaves of Autumn

Nikita Gill (b. 1987)

Between hot chocolate and pumpkin spice,
mellow warmth and misty mornings,

the gold of your mother shines
alongside your father's glowing smile.

Your grandmother bakes buttery cookies,
while your grandfather rakes the amber orange garden.

In a season where everything leaves,
you learn the fine art of loving and letting go.

Yellow October

Sujata Bhatt (b. 1956)

A tree can become like that only in New England's fall,
in Iowa's fall...
Not in Europe's autumn.

This maple made its own light:
clear yellow
as if its sap were singing,
smouldering alert
and preparing itself for something beyond winter.

Of course, I thought it was the moon at first –
but the moon was a sharp bitten off
punky earring that night.
There were no street lamps
and the wide Iowa houses stayed heavily dark
with their 2:00 a.m. privacy.
So the tree made its own light
as if preparing itself to speak.

A tree can become like that only in New England's fall,
in Iowa's fall...
Not in Europe's autumn.

This clear yellow light
made me want to stand there
beside it all night, just staring up the trunk.
And it even felt warm there, so I thought
I could easily sleep beneath
the saxifrage-amber,
lively bright leaves, clean and inquiring
as a young giraffe's wet eyes.
I wanted to sleep beside that strength,
to sleep with that tree, that yellow –

Leaves

Ted Hughes (1930–1998)

Who's killed the leaves?
Me, says the apple, I've killed them all.
Fat as a bomb or a cannonball
I've killed the leaves.

Who sees them drop?
Me, says the pear, they will leave me all bare
So all the people can point and stare.
I see them drop.

Who'll catch their blood?
Me, me, me, says the marrow, the marrow.
I'll get so rotund that they'll need a wheelbarrow.
I'll catch their blood.

Who'll make their shroud?
Me, says the swallow, there's just time enough
Before I must pack all my spools and be off.
I'll make their shroud.

Who'll dig their grave?
Me, says the river, with the power of the clouds
A brown deep grave I'll dig under my floods.
I'll dig their grave.

Who'll be their parson?
Me, says the Crow, for it is well known
I study the bible right down to the bone.
I'll be their parson.

Who'll be chief mourner?
Me, says the wind, I'll cry through the grass
The people will pale and go cold when I pass.
I'll be chief mourner.

Who'll carry the coffin?
Me, says the sunset, the whole world will weep
To see me lower it into the deep.
I'll carry the coffin.

Who'll sing a psalm?
Me, says the tractor, with my gear-grinding glottle
I'll plough up the stubble and sing through my throttle.
I'll sing the psalm.

Who'll toll the bell?
Me, says the robin, my song in October
Will tell the still gardens the leaves are over.
I'll toll the bell.

At Day-Close in November

Thomas Hardy (1840–1928)

The ten hours' light is abating,
    And a late bird wings across,
Where the pines, like waltzers waiting,
    Give their black heads a toss.

Beech leaves, that yellow the noon-time,
    Float past like specks in the eye;
I set every tree in my June time,
    And now they obscure the sky.

And the children who ramble through here
    Conceive that there never has been
A time when no tall trees grew here,
    That none will in time be seen.

little tree

E. E. Cummings (1894–1962)

little tree
little silent Christmas tree
you are so little
you are more like a flower

who found you in the green forest
and were you very sorry to come away?
see   i will comfort you
because you smell so sweetly

i will kiss your cool bark
and hug you safe and tight
just as your mother would,
only don't be afraid

look   the spangles
that sleep all the year in a dark box
dreaming of being taken out and allowed to shine,
the balls the chains red and gold the fluffy threads,

put up your little arms
and i'll give them all to you to hold
every finger shall have its ring
and there won't be a single place dark or unhappy

then when you're quite dressed
you'll stand in the window for everyone to see
and how they'll stare!
oh but you'll be very proud

and my little sister and i will take hands
and looking up at our beautiful tree
we'll dance and sing
'Noel Noel'

The Way Home

Liz Berry (b. 1980)

Take me among the poplars
where beeches surrender to a path of gold;
before the silver birch,
its slender body tongued by the mouth of dusk.
Take my hand in yours as the path disappears
and do not turn from me
when I kneel to bury my old life in the wet earth,
the life I wept for those nights, the one I dreamt I would
    lose.

For our boy is waiting inside me,
his love a green bud, and nothing matters now but this,
this autumn afternoon in a singing copse
where we will lay ourselves down
like copper leaves,
that he may never step upon anything but light.

The Year's Midnight

Gillian Clarke (b. 1937)

The flown, the fallen,
the golden ones,
the deciduous dead, all gone
to ground, to dust, to sand,
borne on the shoulders of the wind.

Listen! They are whispering
now while the world talks,
and the ice melts,
and the seas rise.
Look at the trees!

Every leaf-scar is a bud
expecting a future.
The earth speaks in parables.
The burning bush. The rainbow.
Promises. Promises.

Abele

Di Slaney

I want to be composted here when I die,
somewhere between the white poplars in my
own Elysian field. Years of sweat will turn my hair
the colour of their leaves like Hercules escaping the lair
of Cacus. A cardboard coffin will do, but please
don't burn me; I want to rot down slowly, tease
the worms and beetles with my juices, tempt
sucking roots to wriggle over my straying, unkempt
bones. You can tuck some keepsakes in beside me,
a few idle things to while away the time. Three
at most, there must be room for my dishevelled skin
to drop and slough away. Then when it's time to begin
again without me, don't cry. When you see
Diana in the sky, milky opals gleaming on the hill, be
glad I'm home forever at the base of such a tree.

The Olive Tree

Lorentzos Mavilis (1860–1912)

In your hollow, nests a swarm of bees,
Old olive tree – you who are bowed beneath
A little green as yet, scant olive wreath –
As if they would intone your obsequies.

And every little bird, tipsy with love,
Chirruping among the boughs above,
Begins to give chase in their amorous bower,
Your branches that will no more come in flower.

How, at your dying, they will fill your arms
With their enchanting noise, and all the charms,
The liveliness, the loveliness, of youth,

Crowding your heart like memories. In truth,
I wish that souls could perish as you do –
The souls that are the sister souls to you.

Sonnet 29

Elizabeth Barrett Browning (1806–1861)

I *think* of thee! – my thoughts do twine and bud
About thee, as wild vines, about a tree,
Put out broad leaves, and soon there's nought to see
Except the straggling green which hides the wood.
Yet, O my palm-tree, be it understood
I will not have my thoughts instead of thee
Who art dearer, better! rather, instantly
Renew thy presence. As a strong tree should,
Rustle thy boughs and set thy trunk all bare,
And let these bands of greenery which insphere thee,
Drop heavily down,... burst, shattered, everywhere!
Because, in this deep joy to see and hear thee
And breathe within thy shadow a new air,
I do not think of thee – I am too near thee.

To the Wayfarer

Anon

I am the heat of your hearth on the cold winter nights, the
friendly
shade screening you from the summer sun, and my fruits
are
refreshing draughts quenching your thirst as you journey
on.

I am the beam that holds your house, the board of your table,
the bed
on which you lie, and the timber that builds your boat.

I am the handle of your hoe, the door of your homestead, the
wood of
your cradle, and the shell of your coffin.

I am the bread of kindness and the flower of beauty. Ye who
pass by,
listen to my prayer: Harm me not.

Credits

Plant a Tree – Lucy Larcom, c.1891

On Forgetting That I Am a Tree – Ruth Awolola, from *Rising Stars New Young Voices in Poetry*, Otter-Barry Books (Reproduced with permission from R. Awolola);

Loveliest of Trees, the Cherry Now – A. E. Housman, from *A Shropshire Lad*, 1896

Extract from Oak – Katharine Towers, from *Oak*, Picador, 2021 (Reproduced with permission of Pan Macmillan through PLS Clear)

Leaving Messages in Trees – Helen Burke, from *Today The Birds Will Sing*, Valley Press, 2016 (Reproduced with permission from Valley Press); Green Rain – Mary Webb, from *Come Hither*, ed. Walter de la Mare, 1923

Moved by the Beauty of Trees – Ishion Hutchinson, from *House of Lords and Commons*. Copyright © 2016 by Ishion Hutchinson. (Reprinted by permission of Farrar, Straus and Giroux. All Rights Reserved. Reproduced with permission from Faber and Faber Ltd)

Untitled – Anryū Suharu, translated by Kenneth Rexroth and Ikuko Atsumi, from *Women Poets of Japan*, copyright © 1973 Kenneth Rexroth and Ikuko Atsumi (Reprinted by permission of New Directions Publishing Corp.)

Extract from The Recollection – Percy Bysshe Shelley, The Pine Forest of the Cascine, near Pisa, To Jane: The Invitation, from *The Recollection*, Percy Bysshe Shelley, *Posthumous Poems*, 1824

Trees – Alfred Joyce Kilmer, from *Trees and Other Poems*, 1914; The Awakening – Anna Wickham, from *The Man with a Hammer*, 1916

The Purple Peach Tree – Su Tung P'o, translated by Kenneth Rexroth, from *One Hundred Poems from the Chinese*, copyright © 1971 Kenneth Rexroth (Reprinted by permission of New Directions Publishing Corp.)

Child's Song in Spring – Edith Nesbit, from *Lavender, in A Pomander of Verse*, 1895

Under Silver How – Sarah Doyle, from *Something so wild and new in this feeling*, V Press, 2021. Poem created from Dorothy Wordsworth's Journals. (Reproduced with permission from S. Doyle)

In May – Alison Brackenbury, from *Skies*, Carcanet Press, 2016 (Reproduced with permission from Carcanet Press)

Listening to the Trees – Mandy Haggith (Reproduced with permission from M. Haggith)

I Saw in Louisiana a Live-Oak Growing – Walt Whitman, from *Leaves of Grass*, 1892

The Trees – Philip Larkin, from *The Complete Poems of Philip Larkin*, ed. Archie Burnett. Copyright © 2012 by The Estate of Philip Larkin (Reprinted by permission of Farrar, Straus and Giroux. All Rights Reserved. Reproduced with permission from Faber and Faber Ltd); Not Dead – Robert Graves, from *Fairies and Fusiliers*, 1918 (Reproduced with permission from Carcanet Press)

Staying Overnight at Xiaosha Stream – Yang Wanli, translated by Jonathan Chaves (Reproduced with permission from J. Chaves)

Climbing – Amy Lowell, from *A Dome of Many-Coloured Glass*, 1912

Trees of Song – Pascale Petit, from *Tiger Girl*, Bloodaxe Books, 2020 (Reproduced with permission of Bloodaxe Books)

In My Garden – Charles Causley, from *I Had a Little Cat: Collected Poems for Children*, Macmillan, 2009 (Reproduced with permission from David Higham Associates Limited)

The Trees' Counselling – Christina Rossetti, from *Midsummer Flowers*, ed. Mary Howitt, Lindsay & Blakiston, 1854

Wind in the Beechwood – Siegfried Sassoon, from *The Old Huntsman and Other Poems*, 1918 © Siegfried Sassoon (Reproduced by kind permission of the Estate of George Sassoon)

The Green Roads – Edward Thomas, from *Poems*, Selwyn & Blount, 1917 (Reproduced with permission from RBH Vellender on behalf of the Estate of Edward Thomas)

The World of Trees – Jackie Kay, from *Darling: New & Selected Poems*, Bloodaxe Books, 2007 (Reproduced with permission of Bloodaxe Books)

Forest – Carol Ann Duffy, from *Collected Poems*, Picador. Copyright © Carol Ann Duffy (Reproduced by permission of the author c/o Rogers, Coleridge & White Ltd., 20 Powis Mews, London W11 1JN)

The Way Through the Woods – Rudyard Kipling, from *Rewards and Fairies*, 1910

Emerson – Mary Mapes Dodge, from *An American Anthology, 1787–1900*, ed. Edmund Clarence Stedman, 1900

Extract from The Marshes of Glynn – Sidney Lanier, #IV from *Hymns of the Marshes*, 1912

The Hollow Wood – Edward Thomas, from *Last Poems*, 1918 (Reproduced with permission from RBH Vellender on behalf of the Estate of Edward Thomas)

Ash-boughs – Gerard Manley Hopkins, from *Poems*, 1918

In the Woods – Kathryn Simmonds, from *The Visitations*, Seren, 2013 Copyright © Kathryn Simmonds (Reproduced by permission of the author c/o Rogers, Coleridge & White Ltd., 20 Powis Mews, W11 1JN

My Orcha'd in Linden Lea – William Barnes, from *Hwomely Rhymes: A Second Collection of Poems in The Dorset Dialect*, 1859

Fall, Leaves, Fall – Emily Brontë, from *The Complete Poems of Emily Brontë*, ed. Clement King Shorter, Hodder & Stoughton, 1908

From Blossoms – Li-Young Lee, from *Rose*. Copyright © 1986 by Li-Young Lee (Reprinted with the permission of The Permissions Company, LLC on behalf of BOA Editions, Ltd., boaeditions.org)

Flowers and Trees – Sir Walter Scott, from *The Lady of the Lake: The Western Waves of Ebbing Day*, John Ballantyne and Co., 1810

Summer Night, Riverside – Sara Teasdale, from *Rivers to the Sea*, The Macmillan Company, 1915

The Beech Tree – Michael Longley, from *Weather in Japan*, Jonathan Cape. Copyright © Michael Longley 2000 (Reprinted by permission of The Random House Group Limited)

Under the Greenwood Tree – William Shakespeare version from *Comedies, Histories, & Tragedies*, Iaggard & Blount, 1923

Climbing Trees – Jason Allen-Paisant, from *Thinking With Trees*, Carcanet, 2021 (Reproduced with permission from Carcanet Press)

The Trees – Jericho Brown, from *The Tradition*. Copyright © 2019 by Jericho Brown (Reprinted with the permission of The Permissions Company, LLC on behalf of Copper Canyon Press, coppercanyonpress.org; Reproduced with permission of Pan Macmillan through PLS Clear)

Extract from The Wanderer – William Wordsworth, from *The Excursion*, 1814

The Trees Outside My Window –Moniza Alvi, from *Split World: Poems 1990–2005*, Bloodaxe Books, 2008 (Reproduced with permission of Bloodaxe Books)

Orchard – Stephen Keeler, unpublished (Reproduced with permission from S. Keeler)

Driving Back Over the Blue Ridge, – Moya Cannon, from *Hands*, Carcanet Press, 2011 (Reproduced with permission from Carcanet Press)

For Catherine © Jen Feroze, from *The Colour of Hope*, self-published (Reproduced with permission from J. Feroze)

There is a Solemn Wind To-Night – Katherine Mansfield, from *Poems 1917-1919*, Constable & Co., 1923

On the First Leaves of Autumn (9 lines) – Nikita Gill, from *These are the Words*, Children's Books, 2022 © Nikita Gill, 2022 (Reproduced by kind permission by David Higham Associates)

Yellow October – Sujata Bhatt, from *Collected Poems*, Carcanet Press (Reproduced with permission from Carcanet Press)

Leaves – Ted Hughes, from *Collected Poems*. Copyright © 2003 by The Estate of Ted Hughes (Reprinted by permission of Farrar, Straus and Giroux. All Rights Reserved. Reproduced with permission from Faber and Faber Ltd)

At Day-Close in November – Thomas Hardy, from *Satires of Circumstance, Lyrics and Reveries with Miscellaneous Pieces*, 1914

little tree – E.E. Cummings. Copyright 1925, 1953, © 1991 by the Trustees for the E. E. Cummings Trust. Copyright © 1976 by George James Firmage, from *Complete Poems: 1904-1962* by E. E. Cummings, ed. George J. Firmage (Used by permission of Liveright Publishing Corporation)

The Way Home – Liz Berry, from *The Republic of Motherhood*, Chatto Windus. Copyright © Liz Berry 2018 (Reprinted by permission of The Random House Group Limited)

The Year's Midnight – Gillian Clarke, from *Collected Poems*, Carcanet (Reproduced with permission from Carcanet Press)

Abele – Di Slaney © Di Slaney, first published *Brittle Star* magazine (Reproduced with permission from D. Slaney)

The Olive Tree – Lorentzos Mavilis, translated by Alicia E. Stallings (Reproduced with permission from A. E. Stallings)

Sonnet 29 – Elizabeth Barrett Browning, from *Sonnets from the Portuguese, Poems*, 1850

To the Wayfarer – Anon, as found in *Spanish Sunshine*, Eleanor Elsner, Century Company, 1925